Nuclear Waste and Radioactivity

Design: David West
                     Children's Book Design
Editor: Roger Vlitos
Editorial planning: Clark Robinson Ltd
Illustrator: Ian Moores
Picture research: Cecilia Weston-Baker
Photographic Credits:
Cover and pages 9 top and bottom, 17 top and bottom and 25 top: Rex
Features; pages 4-5 and 15 bottom: Frank Spooner Agency; pages 6, 11 right,
19, 20, 21, 23 both, 25 bottom and 28: Science Photo Library; pages 12, 13
and 24: Hutchison Library; page 27 top: J. Allan Cash Library; pages 27
bottom and 29 both: Topham Picture Library.

Created and designed by
Aladdin Books Ltd
70 Old Compton Street
London W1V 5PA

A CIP catalogue record for this book
is available from the British Library

First published in
Great Britain in 1990 by
Gloucester Press
96 Leonard Street
London EC2A 4RH

ISBN 0-7496-0123-X

Printed in Belgium

The publishers would like to acknowledge that the photographs reproduced
within this book have been posed by models or have been obtained from
photographic agencies.

Facts on

Nuclear Waste and Radioactivity

Hugh Johnstone

GLOUCESTER PRESS

London · New York · Toronto · Sydney

CONTENTS

INTRODUCTION

When the first nuclear power stations were opened in the 1950s their technology was heralded as one of the great achievements of modern science. Nowadays many people fear nuclear power is a costly mistake which may cause great problems for our planet. However, provided they are treated with great care and respect, nuclear materials offer us many benefits. There may still be the prospect of safe and well controlled power, while the other great application of nuclear energy is the use of radiation in medicine. Steady progress in this field means that we can now detect and treat serious diseases, including cancer.

There are many fears about nuclear power. Some people call it "unnatural" even though the light and heat we receive daily from the sun is the result of a thermonuclear reaction. It is important to understand the nature of nuclear energy and the modern technology we use to harness it. We must also learn from past mistakes and not let our fears blind us to whatever potential for progress still exists. One thing is certain , we are all now living in what people call "the nuclear age".

WHAT IS RADIATION ?

Radiation in various forms is around us all the time. Common examples are heat, sunlight and radio waves. Nuclear radiation and X-rays are a special type called ionising radiation which we have to control because it can be harmful. Although our senses will not alert us to its presence, this sort of radiation can be detected using special instruments and we can measure the amount to which a person has been exposed. The radiation produced by radioactive materials normally consists of alpha and beta particles and gamma rays. Alpha and beta particles are fragments of atoms broken free and shot out by the energy of atomic reactions. Gamma rays are similar to X-rays and both of them are a form of electromagnetic radiation like light-rays.

HELPFUL X-RAYS

In most countries X-rays are the main type of artificial radiation to which people are exposed. These rays can pass right through the body and are used by doctors to check for disease and injuries such as broken bones. However, the amount of X-ray exposure has to be kept very small since large doses of radiation are harmful. X-rays also have important industrial uses such as checking parts for internal damage.

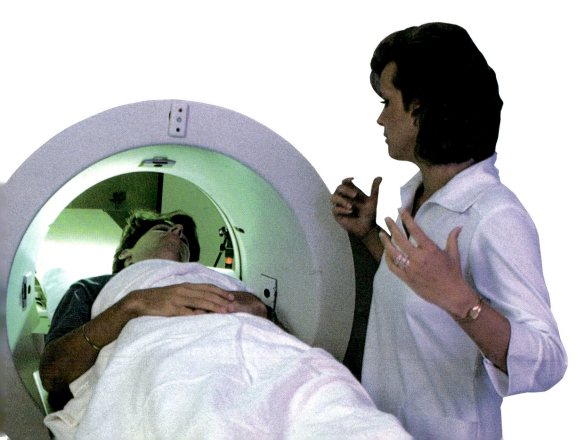

BLOCKING RADIATION

Radiation can be controlled by enclosing the sources with shielding to absorb the particles or waves. Alpha particles only have a weak penetrating power and can be stopped by a sheet of paper. They cannot penetrate the skin. Beta particles penetrate more strongly but can be stopped by a solid object like a thin sheet of aluminium. Gamma rays have the greatest penetrating power and much heavier shielding like lead, steel sheet, or concrete is needed to reduce their intensity to a safe level.

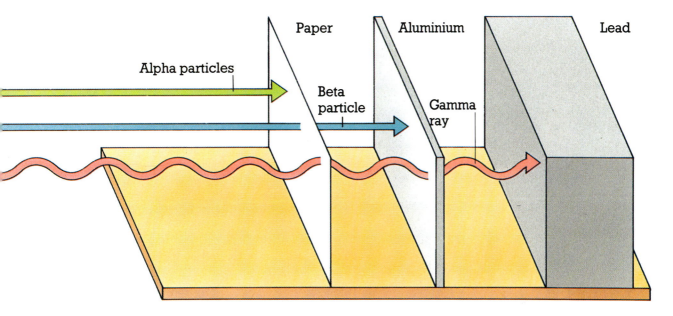

Paper

Aluminium

Lead

Alpha particles

Beta particle

Gamma ray

POISON!

Exposure to large amounts of penetrating radiation like X-rays or gamma rays causes radiation sickness. Very high radiation levels can kill a person within a few hours or days. It destroys the body's central nervous system, which soon leads to collapse or death. A low level of radiation over a long period of time will not cause radiation sickness but – depending on the intensity – can harm the body's vital blood-producing cells. Cancer and leukemias can develop depending on the total radiation dose absorbed by the body.

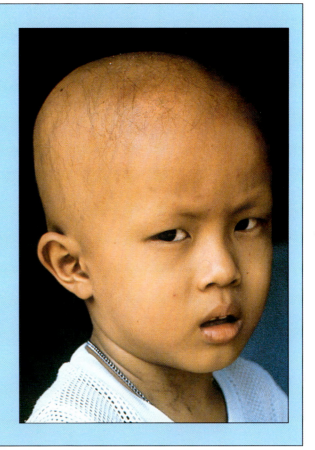

NUCLEAR REACTIONS

The energy in nuclear reactors is produced by splitting atoms. These are the tiny particles of which all matter is made. Atoms consist of an outer layer of electrons surrounding a central core. This core is the nucleus which contains two kinds of particles, called protons and neutrons. The number of protons varies according to which element the atom belongs. There are two types of nuclear reaction, fission and fusion. In fission the atomic nucleus is broken up into two lighter nuclei of around the same size. In fusion two nuclei are joined together to form just one nucleus. Both of these reactions produce atoms of different elements. During either reaction only a small fraction of the material from the original atoms is converted into heat and energy including radiation. Nuclear fission is the method used in most power stations.

NUCLEAR FUSION

Fusion involves the joining of two atoms, such as deuterium and tritium which are isotopes of the element hydrogen. If two of these nuclei can be brought close enough together they will fuse to produce a single helium atom.

The fusion of tritium and deuterium produces helium which releases heat and radiation energy.

However there is a natural repulsion between the nuclei which makes it very difficult to produce a continuous controlled fusion reaction.

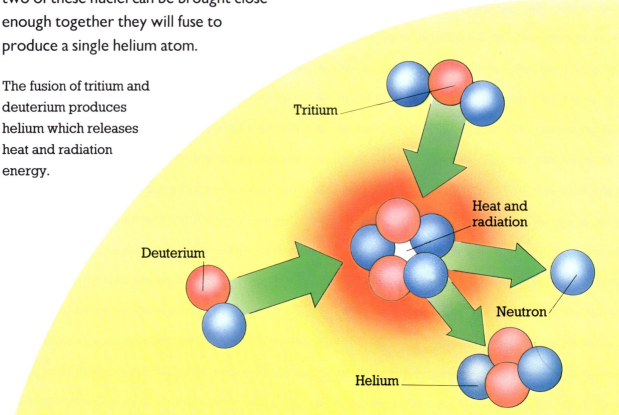

Tritium

Deuterium

Heat and radiation

Neutron

Helium

NUCLEAR FISSION

Uranium has the largest natural atoms and if a uranium nucleus is struck by a neutron it may undergo fission, splitting into two parts. There are three types of uranium atom, or isotopes, with Uranium-235 being the one that undergoes fission most easily. The fission process produces heat and gives off additional neutrons. If there are enough uranium atoms close together the neutrons produced by the fission of one atom can shoot into the nucleus of another atom and make it undergo fission. If the process continues repeating a chain reaction results. In atom bombs a chain reaction is allowed to build up very quickly and the immense amount of energy released gives a huge explosion.

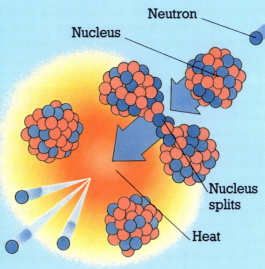

Neutron

Nucleus

Nucleus splits

Heat

The picture above shows damage done to Hiroshima by an atomic bomb.

NUCLEAR POWER

The heart of a nuclear power station is the reactor. Here a controlled nuclear fission reaction produces a lot of heat. This heat is carried away by a coolant circulating through the reactor core and then used to generate steam. The steam drives turbines to generate electricity in the same way as a conventional power station. There are several different types of reactor, the most common being the pressurised water reactor. In this design the cooling water is kept under pressure to prevent it boiling and to give higher working temperatures. The hot coolant is pumped to a heat exchanger where it boils a separate supply of water which produces radiation-free steam for the turbines. New ideas for producing energy from nuclear fusion are still being developed.

HOW THEY WORK

Control of the chain reaction in a reactor is achieved using control rods that absorb neutrons. When the rods are lowered into the core, free neutrons are soaked up so they are unable to start fission reactions in the uranium atoms.

As the control rods are withdrawn fewer of the neutrons are absorbed, leaving more to start fission. The reactor is said to "go critical" (it becomes self-sustaining) when one of the neutrons from each fission reaction manages to start another reaction.

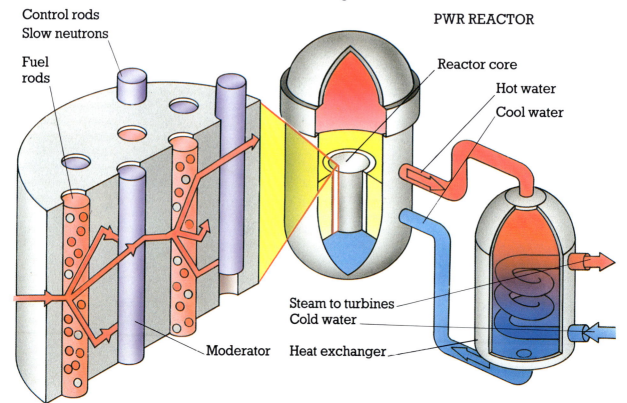

Control rods
Slow neutrons

Fuel rods

PWR REACTOR

Reactor core

Hot water

Cool water

Steam to turbines
Cold water

Moderator   Heat exchanger

WHAT THEY LOOK LIKE

The reactor of a modern power station is enclosed in a gas-tight containment structure designed to withstand high pressures and temperatures, and to trap any radioactivity released in the event of a reactor failure. In some designs of nuclear power station this protective structure is clearly visible as a separate dome. Inside there is little sign of the nuclear reactor which is sealed away in a steel and concrete reactor vessel, and biological shield, to prevent the escape of radiation.

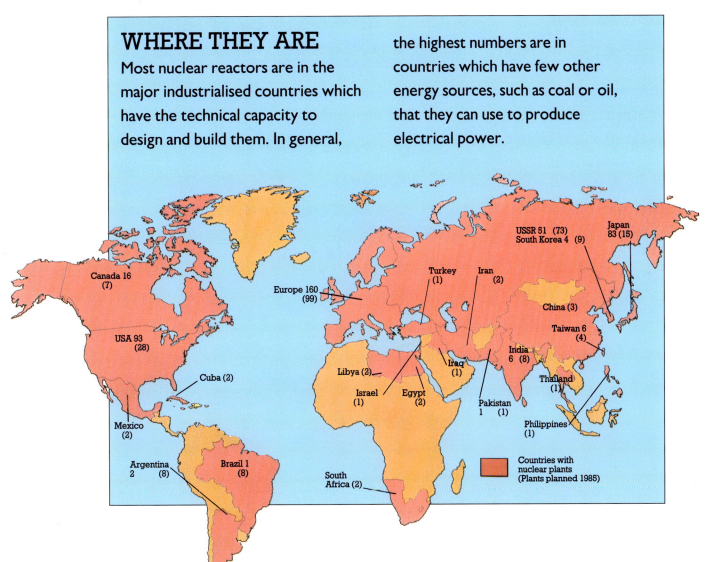

WHERE THEY ARE

Most nuclear reactors are in the major industrialised countries which have the technical capacity to design and build them. In general, the highest numbers are in countries which have few other energy sources, such as coal or oil, that they can use to produce electrical power.

Canada 16 (7)

Europe 160 (99)

USA 93 (28)

Cuba (2)

Mexico (2)

Argentina 2 (8)

Brazil 1 (8)

South Africa (2)

Turkey (1)

Iran (2)

Libya (2)

Israel (1)

Egypt (2)

Iraq (1)

Pakistan 1 (1)

India 6 (8)

USSR 51 (73)

South Korea 4 (9)

Japan 83 (15)

China (3)

Taiwan 6 (4)

Thailand (1)

Philippines (1)

Countries with nuclear plants (Plants planned 1985)

DANGERS – MINING

Most nuclear reactors use uranium for fuel and there are large deposits of uranium ore in only a few places around the world. These ores only contain a small proportion of uranium, on average about 0.13 per cent, so the mined ore has to be concentrated. To do this it is ground up and chemically treated to give a mixture of uranium oxides called "yellowcake" which contains around 75 per cent uranium. Less than one per cent of the yellowcake consists of the fissile U-235 isotope. Uranium ores are not highly radioactive but particular dangers are posed by the presence of a naturally occuring gas called radon, which is produced by radioactive decay of uranium. Crushing the ore releases poisonous radon gas which has been trapped within the rock.

IN THE '50s

During the 1950s the high demand for uranium for military purposes, and later for power reactors, created a uranium mining boom. Ore deposits were mined in the same way as any other minerals with little attention being paid to the risks of radioactivity. High radon levels were common in underground mines with poor ventilation and many miners developed lung cancer from breathing the dangerous radioactive gas.

MODERN DAY

Modern uranium mines are generally large scale operations using both open-cast and underground mining methods. These basic mining techniques are the same as for other minerals but particular care is taken to avoid radiation leakage and to provide good ventilation. The waste products, or "tailings", as they are called, contain most of the radioactivity. They are often reburied in worked-out parts of a mine.

HOUSING

The tailings left when uranium is extracted from its ore contain radium produced by natural uranium fission. Radium is a dangerously radioactive material that decays to produce radon gas. Tailings from early uranium mines were often left about or even used as landfill under houses. This created serious pollution and in some areas the tailings have had to be removed and buildings evacuated.

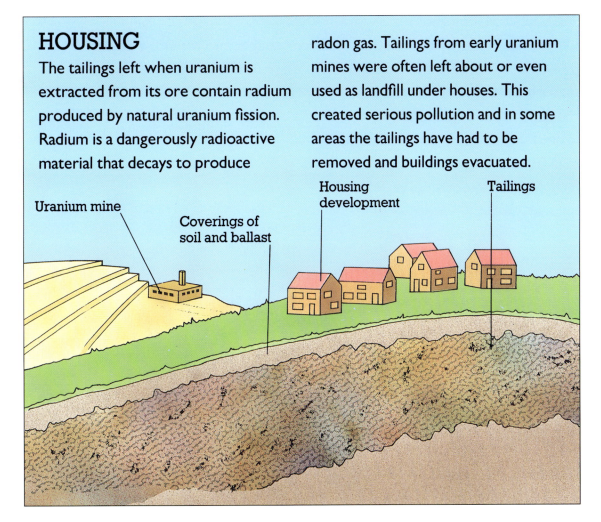

Uranium mine

Coverings of soil and ballast

Housing development

Tailings

DANGERS – LEAKS

We cannot see, feel or smell nuclear radiation and to many people this makes it seem much more threatening. Some of the greatest worries are about the risk of accidental or deliberate releases of radioactive materials from nuclear power stations and fuel reprocessing plants. Both power stations and reprocessing plants discharge limited amounts of radioactive materials during normal operation. These discharges are of radioactive gases into the atmosphere and low-level liquid wastes pumped out to sea. Strict limits are set for the amount of material that can be discharged in these ways to make sure local radioactivity is kept well within agreed levels. However, these limits are sometimes exceeded. As a result many people refuse to live near nuclear reactors.

PROTEST

Unease about the safety of nuclear power has often been expressed in public protests. These range from the activities of environmental groups such as Greenpeace who concentrate attention on specific dangers like the discharge of nuclear waste from processing plants to major public protests against the construction of power stations. Legal and political methods are also used by protest groups. In the USA public worries about the safety of nuclear power stations, combined with increasing cost, has stopped the development of nuclear power since the accident at the Three Mile Island plant. No new stations have been ordered and some scheduled plants have not been brought into use while others have been left half finished.

CONTAMINATION

Sensitive instruments can measure very low levels of radioactivity from waste discharges and accidental releases. Regular checks are made by power and reprocessing plants, and by anti-nuclear organisations. Sometimes the measurements help protesters prove that plants are discharging excessive amounts of radioactivity.

DANGERS – ACCIDENTS

Even more worrying than the possibility of nuclear leaks is the risk of a major nuclear reactor accident releasing large amounts of radioactivity into the environment or causing a nuclear explosion. In practice the main risk is from a core meltdown where the reactor cooling system fails and the core heats up enough for the fuel to melt and run down into the bottom of the reactor. As a safety precaution, reactors have emergency cooling systems and reinforced containment structures to prevent the escape of radioactive materials even if there is a failure of the system. Several serious accidents have occurred, but with the exception of Chernobyl, there have not been any major releases of radioactivity from nuclear power stations as yet. This fact, say some protest groups, only creates a sense of false confidence.

CHINA SYNDROME

The phrase *China syndrome* relates to a myth about faulty nuclear reactors and it became famous as the title of a popular film. The core of an out of control nuclear reactor is supposed to become so hot that it can melt its way right through the earth to come out in China! Such a catastrophic failure could not actually occur. The heated mass would simply spread out into the surrounding ground. The main problems would be the contamination of the area and underground water supplies.

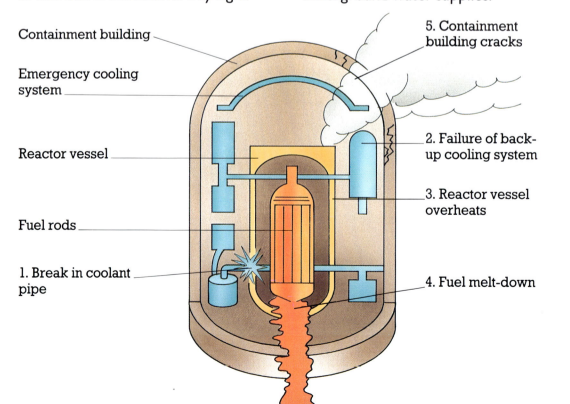

Containment building

Emergency cooling system

Reactor vessel

Fuel rods

1. Break in coolant pipe

5. Containment building cracks

2. Failure of back-up cooling system

3. Reactor vessel overheats

4. Fuel melt-down

EVACUATION

As part of their safety systems nuclear power stations and reprocessing plants have emergency plans to deal with accidents. If released radioactivity starts to approach a dangerous level, people living and working in the affected area will be evacuated under the guidance of local emergency services. They will be allowed to return only after the area has been thoroughly checked to make sure the radiation levels are safe.

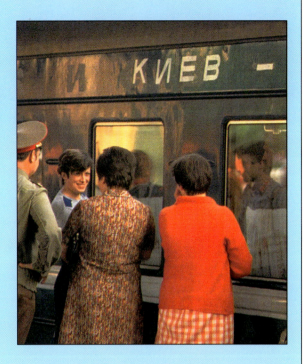

CHERNOBYL

A major nuclear accident occurred at the Chernobyl power plant in Russia during April 1986. Operators had switched off most of the reactor safety devices when a series of errors caused severe overheating of the core. Core cooling water was instantly turned into steam, giving a huge pressure shock that blew the top off the reactor. This released a cloud of radioactive material that spread right across Europe.

REPROCESSING

Reprocessing is one of the most controversial areas of the nuclear industry. The fission of uranium in a reactor results in a build-up of waste products in the fuel elements. Reprocessing extracts unused, and very valuable, uranium for new fuel. Since all of these materials are highly radioactive the entire operation has to be carried out under remote control. Storage of the waste is particularly tricky and reprocessing plants worldwide have a history of leaks. Evidence points to the fact that leaks have contaminated workers at reprocessing plants as well as people living nearby. One plant in the United States has even been closed because of leaks. Some people now think that all reprocessing should be banned. However, this would put up the cost of nuclear power and increase the amount of dangerous waste in storage.

TRANSPORTATION

Reprocessing of nuclear fuel is carried out at specialised plants and used fuel elements have to be transported there from the power stations. Radioactive fuel elements are carried in big steel flasks, which may also be lead lined to give radiation shielding and protection against accidental leakage. These flasks can weigh up to 110 tonnes and have to meet international regulations to make sure they will withstand accidents and fires. In one spectacular demonstration the strength of a British fuel flask was tested by crashing a diesel locomotive into it at a speed of 90mph. The locomotive was destroyed but the flask remained sealed although it had been dented. Such flasks are carried by either road, rail, or specially designed ships to their destinations around the world.

FUEL CYCLE

After removal from the reactor, fuel elements are stored in cooling ponds to let the initial high radiation die down. They are then transported to the reprocessing plant. Here the metal casings are removed and the fuel dissolved in nitric acid. Waste products are chemically removed from the solution and the uranium recovered for processing into new fuel elements. Plutonium is also recovered and may be used as fuel for fast breeder reactors. The waste products are radioactive and have to be stored in special shielded tanks.

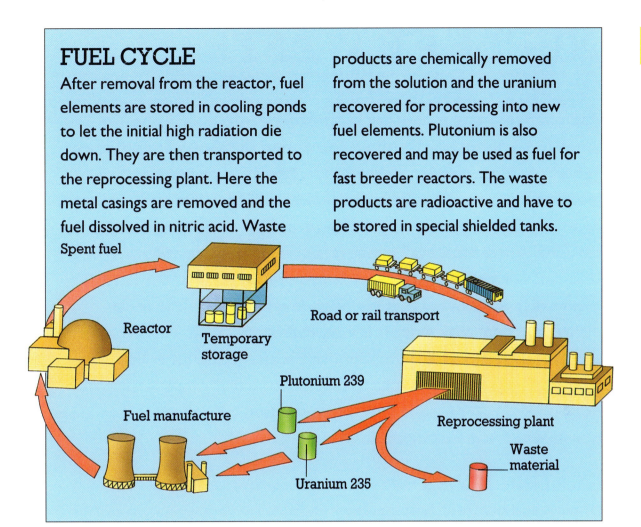

Spent fuel

Reactor

Temporary storage

Road or rail transport

Fuel manufacture

Plutonium 239

Uranium 235

Reprocessing plant

Waste material

NUCLEAR WASTE

Radioactive waste is another big problem with nuclear power since it has to be disposed of without increasing the risks of exposure to radiation. Most nuclear waste is "low-level", such as overalls and gloves which are only slightly radioactive. These are sealed in steel drums and buried in concrete-lined trenches or underground caverns. "Intermediate" waste is more radioactive and must be shielded during handling. Most is now stored at nuclear plants for future disposal underground. "High-level" waste is the most difficult to deal with since it is very radioactive and will remain so for hundreds of years. At present this waste is stored as liquid in special containers which has to be cooled so that the contents do not boil away. A possible long-term solution is to convert it to glass blocks which can be buried deep underground.

EXISTING HOLES

Underground storage is used for nuclear waste because the earth acts as an extra radiation shield and the waste is less likely to be disturbed. Some old mines are suitable for use as waste depositories. Salt mines are particularly suitable because they are dry, deep, and because salt can absorb some radiation. Low and intermediate level waste is encased in concrete and stacked in caverns within the mine. They are then covered with salt and the caverns are closed off when they are full.

UNDERGROUND STORAGE

Long-term storage of nuclear waste relies on the use of multiple barriers to prevent radiation escapes. One possible type of underground disposal centre would have a series of chambers dug deep in ground that has been checked to make sure it is free from geological faults. The chambers would be at least 200ft below the surface. Waste packed in steel drums and covered in concrete would be loaded into outer cases and stacked in the chambers. The space round the cases would have to be packed with concrete or earth and the filled chambers sealed off.

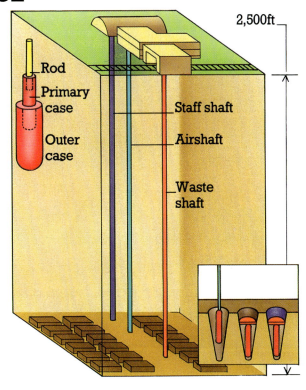

Rod
Primary case
Outer case
Staff shaft
Airshaft
Waste shaft
2,500ft

STORED IN GLASS

High-level radioactive waste is normally stored in liquid form. This can be reduced in volume by a process called *vitrification* which converts it into a glass-like substance. We can see this red-hot "glass" being poured into a steel drum in the picture below.

After a very long time it is possible for small amounts of radioactive waste to be dissolved out of this substance by water. In Australia another storage technique has been invented which seems safer. High-level radioactive waste is converted into a rock-like substance called synrock.

USES IN MEDICINE

One of the first uses of radiation was in medicine, and medicine is the largest source of man-made radiation for most of us. Most common are **X**-rays, but continued technical improvements have considerably reduced the amount of radiation exposure needed for each picture. Direct use of radioactive materials is also widespread in medicine. Some are used as a source of gamma rays for the radiation treatment of cancers and tumours. Others are used for making radiographic images similar to **X**-rays but capable of providing different details of information. Radioactive isotopes of many different substances are produced by exposing them to radiation and used for direct treatment or for finding out if something is wrong internally with a patient.

TRACING DISEASE

Radioactive tracers make it possible to take pictures of specific organs and check how they are working. The patient is given a dose of the tracer which circulates through the body and becomes concentrated in specific organs. By using different tracers the doctors can examine the workings of selected organs. Tracers emit gamma rays which are detected by a gamma ray camera positioned over the patient. The camera converts the radiation to flashes of light which give a much stronger signal to the detectors (see diagram below).

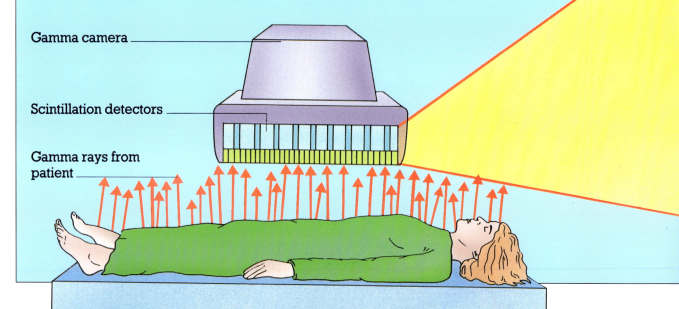

Gamma camera

Scintillation detectors

Gamma rays from patient

FIGHTING DISEASE

Radiotherapy destroys cancers by giving them high doses of radiation. To minimise damage to other cells the radiation has to be closely focused on the cancer. Beta and gamma rays from radioactive sources and high power X-rays are used. Another way of applying the radiation is to implant radioactive materials into the cancer. Radiotherapy can have unpleasant side-effects and sometimes only prolongs life by a few months or years. Still, there is hope that results will improve.

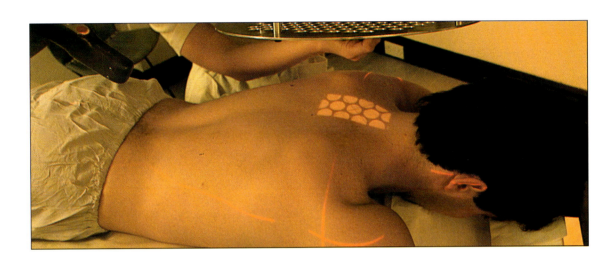

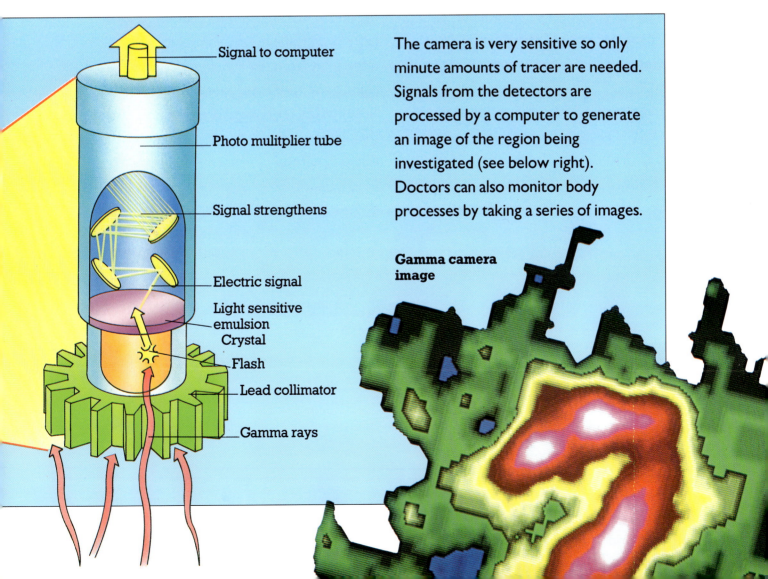

Signal to computer

Photo mulitplier tube

Signal strengthens

Electric signal

Light sensitive emulsion
Crystal

Flash

Lead collimator

Gamma rays

The camera is very sensitive so only minute amounts of tracer are needed. Signals from the detectors are processed by a computer to generate an image of the region being investigated (see below right). Doctors can also monitor body processes by taking a series of images.

Gamma camera image

RISKS COMPARED

Saying that you have much less than one chance in a million of being killed by an accident with a nuclear reactor does not really mean much to most of us. A better guide is given by saying that the risk of being involved in a serious nuclear accident is several thousand times less that that of being run over by a car. Trying to grasp the possible effects of long-term radiation is equally difficult because radiation is naturally present around us. Most of the estimates for the long-term effects of radiation are based on studies of the survivors of the Hiroshima and Nagasaki atomic bombs and may not be typical. But we do know that the radiation levels involved are only a fraction of the natural levels mankind has grown up with.

THE SUN'S RADIATION

The sun produces vast amounts of radiation but the Earth's atmosphere stops most of it from reaching the surface. This also applies to cosmic radiation from the galaxy. Of course visible light gets through fairly easily as does some ultra-violet light (which causes sunburn) and some cosmic radiation. The ozone layer, above 15 km in the atmosphere, absorbs most of the ultraviolet from the sun. People living high up, or who travel often in aircraft, are exposed to higher levels because the thinner atmosphere has less of a shielding effect.

RADON

Radon is a highly radioactive gas formed during the natural decay of uranium. It decays into other radioactive products which like radon itself can be inhaled and trapped in the lungs. This gives a high radiation dose that can cause cancer. In some areas natural radon builds up in houses and other buildings giving a local radioactivity level several times greater than average.

NUCLEAR POWER

Nuclear reactors and fuel recycling plants only produce a fraction of one per cent of the radiation we are exposed to in the world. This will probably grow if more use is made of nuclear power. Accidents may have a greater effect. Chernobyl is estimated to have increased the average UK radiation dose by just less than 20 per cent in the first year.

HOW MUCH

Most of the radiation we are exposed to comes from natural sources, with radiation from the air and from the ground being the major contributors. The food we eat is also slightly radioactive as a result of plants and animals taking up natural radioactive materials from the earth. Fallout from atomic weapons tests is the second largest man-made source of radiation, but has become much smaller since atmospheric tests ceased. However, the effects of Chernobyl are still being assessed.

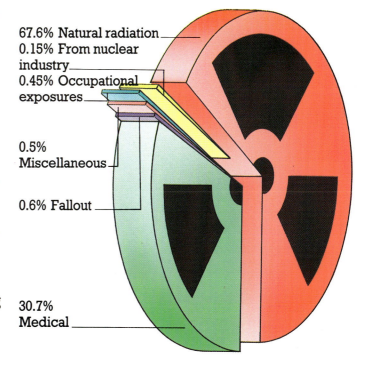

67.6% Natural radiation
0.15% From nuclear industry
0.45% Occupational exposures
0.5% Miscellaneous
0.6% Fallout
30.7% Medical

SAFETY RECORD

The development of nuclear power has been far from trouble free. There have been a number of well publicised accidents, some of them releasing significant amounts of radioactivity to the environment. However the lessons from these accidents have been applied to increase the safety of both new and existing nuclear installations. These extra measures have greatly increased costs, reducing the financial attractions of nuclear power. Another result of these accidents has been the introduction of strict reporting systems for all incidents at nuclear plants, no matter how small. Because of this there has been increased publicity about nuclear accidents even though some members of the industry claim the actual risks have probably been reduced.

WHEN IT GOES WRONG

When the Three Mile Island reactor failed in March 1979 there were conflicting reports about what was happening, and especially about the dangers of radioactive releases. As a safety measure the Governor of Pennsylvania recommended the evacuation of all children and pregnant women within a five mile radius of the plant. Many other people chose to leave the area.

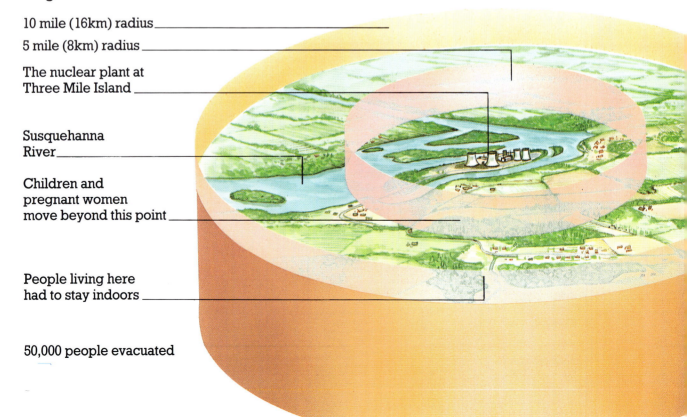

10 mile (16km) radius

5 mile (8km) radius

The nuclear plant at Three Mile Island

Susquehanna River

Children and pregnant women move beyond this point

People living here had to stay indoors

50,000 people evacuated

COAL AND OIL

Coal and oil are familiar fuels that most people accept without any worries but they both involve immediate risks that are a lot higher than those of nuclear energy. As with nuclear power it is workers in the industries that are most likely to suffer. Coal miners are killed every year, and fatal accidents occur on oil rigs. Releases of oil or fuel gases are a real danger to the public. Pollution control laws have reduced some of the worst environmental effects of these fuels, but we are only just starting to realise the accumulative effects such as global warming. It may be that we have no choice but to include nuclear power in our long-term plans.

CONCLUSIONS

Now the initial enthusiasm has waned we realise that nuclear power needs careful, and expensive, controls to ensure public safety and that it has some definite long-term problems. But it also appears that other energy sources, in particular the burning of fossil fuels, have their own problems. Furthermore, fossil fuel resources are not endless and may well run out by the middle of the next century. If we want to go on using energy at anything like the present rate we may well find we have to rely more on nuclear power. But we will have to take all possible steps to make it safe. Other uses of radiation are less likely to cause argument. Few people would want to give up the considerable improvements in diagnosis and treatment that have been achieved by nuclear medicine.

CLEAN AIR

Clean and non-polluting electricity generation is one of the main advantages claimed for nuclear power stations. The absence of smoke and fumes is an obvious advantage of a nuclear power station. But there may be low-level discharges of radioactive materials which will take years to disperse.

AIR POLLUTION

Burning fossil fuels like coal and oil releases carbon dioxide to the air. This is now believed to be a major factor in global warming. Though the details are uncertain this could have very serious effects for the planet with major climatic changes. More direct pollutants, like sulphur dioxide which causes acid rain, are also released though these can be limited by fitting emission control systems.

SPILLAGE

Oil is an efficient fuel but it can also be dangerous. As well as being a fire risk, accidental oil spillage and careless tank-washing cause considerable ecological damage.

NUCLEAR FACTS

Nuclear power produces about 15 per cent of the electricity generated in the world. In some countries research reactors only make a token contribution to the electricity supply. In others such as France nuclear power is the main source of electricity.

Little Boy, the first atomic bomb, was dropped on Hiroshima, Japan, on 6 August 1945.

Percentage of nuclear production per country 1985

Pakistan 0.09
Brazil 1.7
India 2.4
Italy 3.8
South Africa 4.1
Yugoslavia 5.4
Netherlands 6.1
Argentina 10.1
USSR 10.3
East Germany 12
Canada 12.7
Czechoslovakia 14.6
USA 15.5
UK 19.8
Japan 22.4
Hungary 23.6
Spain 24
South Korea 25.9
West Germany 31.2
Bulgaria 32.6
Finland 38.2
Switzerland 39.8
Sweden 42.3
Taiwan 53.1
Belgium 59.8
France 64.8

One tonne of uranium used as fuel for a nuclear reactor can produce as much energy as 20,000 tonnes of coal burnt in an electricity power station.

Radiation doses are measured in millisieverts (mSV) which allow for the biological effects of different types of radiation. The average background radiation is about 2.5 mSv. Sometimes an older measurement, the rem, is used instead. One rem is equal to 10 mSv.

The strength of a radiation source is measured in becquerels (Bq). One becquerel is the activity of a source that has one nuclear disintegration a second.

Major accidents involving the release of nuclear materials from a reactor occurred at Windscale, England in 1957 and at Chernobyl, Russia in 1986. No immediate deaths occurred at Windscale (now known as Sellafield) but around 30 deaths were predicted to be caused by radiation effects. At Chernobyl there were 31 immediate deaths. Radiation released by this accident is expected to cause around 1000 cancer deaths in Europe over the next 40 years.

The Three Mile Island accident at Harrisburg, USA in 1979 involved the melt-down of the reactor core. However the containment structure worked properly and only a small amount of radiation was released.

GLOSSARY

element substance consisting entirely of atoms containing the same number of protons.

fallout radioactive particles created by an atomic explosion and falling from the atmosphere down to the earth's surface.

fission break-up of an atomic nucleus into two smaller parts of approximately the same size usually with the production of neutrons.

half-life time it takes for a sample of radioactive material to lose half its radioactivity by natural decay.

isotopes atoms of the same element but with different numbers of neutrons in their nuclei such as deuterium and tritium.

nucleus (nuclei) core of an atom, made up from protons and neutrons.

plutonium radioactive element with an atomic mass greater than that of uranium.

proton elementary particle forming part of the core of an atom. It has an electric charge .

radio-isotope radioactive isotope of an element.

tailings waste material left after uranium has been mined.

U-235 isotope of uranium that can sustain a nuclear chain reaction.

yellowcake mixture of uranium oxides produced from uranium ore.

Useful addresses

British Nuclear Fuels plc, Risley, Warrington WA3 6AS

Central Electricity Generating Board, Sudbury House, 15 Newgate Street, London EC1A 7AU

The European Community, Radiation and Radiation Protection, 8 Storey's Gate, London SW1P 3AT

Friends of the Earth
26-28 Underwood Street, London N1 7JQ, England
also
218 Dee St SE. Washington DC 20003, USA

Greenpeace, 30-31 Islington Green, London N1

International Atomic Energy Agency. PO Box 100, A-1400 Vienna, Austria

National Radiological Protection Board, Chilton, Didcot, Oxfordshire OX11 0QR

UK Nirex Ltd, Curie Avenue, Harwell, Didcot, Oxfordshire OX11 0RA

United States Nuclear Regulatory Commission, Washington DC 20555, United States

32

INDEX

PRINTED IN BELGIUM BY
proost
INTERNATIONAL BOOK PRODUCTION